POETS NOW

Edited by Robert Peters

PRACTICING TO BE A WOMAN

*New and Selected Poems
by Rochelle Ratner*

Poets Now 2

The Scarecrow Press, Inc.
Metuchen, N.J., & London 1982

Some of these poems have previously appeared in the following magazines: *Flute, Green House, Shantih,* and *Text,* and in the anthology *Loves, Etc.* (Doubleday/Anchor, 1973).

BOOKS BY ROCHELLE RATNER

Poetry

A BIRTHDAY OF WATERS, New Rivers Press, 1971
FALSE TREES, New Rivers Press, 1973
THE MYSTERIES, Ragnarok Press, 1976
PIRATE'S SONG, Jordan Davies Press, 1976
THE TIGHTROPE WALKER, Pennyworth Press, 1977
QUARRY, New Rivers Press, 1978
COMBING THE WAVES, Hanging Loose Press, 1979
HIDE & SEEK, Ommation Press, 1979
SEA AIR IN A GRAVE GROUND HOG TURNS TOWARD,
     'Gull Publications, 1980

Translations

PAUL COLINET: SELECTED PROSE POEMS, Clown War, 1975
SONGS OF THE WOMEN OF FES, Tiresias Press, forthcoming 1982

Library of Congress Cataloging in Publication Data
Ratner, Rochelle
   Practicing to be a woman.

   (Poets now   ; no. 2)
   I. Title.   II. Series.
PS3568.A76P7   811'.54   81-21472
ISBN 0-8108-1510-9   AACR2

C.1

For Elizabeth Marraffino,
John Perlman, and
Nathan Whiting —
with me since the first poems

INTRODUCTION

As one of the very first volumes initiating this series, Rochelle Ratner's *Practicing To Be A Woman* seems especially appropriate for the accessibility of its writing, for the poet's courageous self-examinations, for its explorations of womanhood, and for its stunning closing series of poems based on the famous medieval unicorn tapestries in the Cloisters, New York City. She represents any number of vigorous young talents, male and female, writing today whose performances augur well for American writing.

Ratner is a multitalented poet. She can write poignantly of her own childhood in Atlantic City and growing into womanhood. At the same time she can present voices, characters, who are only tangentially she: she speaks through a mermaid, who like Matthew Arnold's seductress, comes ashore to fulfill some of her destiny as a woman; and she speaks through a unicorn of fantasy who is victim of the royal spears and the royal hounds, a figure of exquisite beauty. Readers will probably find the childhood and other personal poems most accessible and immediately moving. The section on womanhood is somewhat more literary in its explorations of language and forms, and displays Ratner at her most inventive. The mermaid image is in itself a poignant metaphor of the unfulfilled woman; she is unable to bear human children, and the sexual act is itself problematic.

The third section, "Remnant," contains two of her finest poems, "The Hell Doll" and "The Geese Purring." These poems are not directly personal, nor biographical, in the sense that the preceding sections are. They reveal another side to Ratner—her fondness for experimenting with lengthy forms. The final section, "Quarry," anticipates forthcoming works. She obviously feels challenged and comfortable with an ambitious sequence of poems around a vivid theme.

Ratner's appearance, then, is the first of several by young, productive poets who have already created something of a name for their work by publishing in small presses. There is so much issuing from these presses that readers and libraries may not know where to begin to choose from amongst the wealth. In devoting part of our series to selections from poets published by these presses, we hope to be providing a valuable service both for libraries and for the writers. We think you will enjoy and be moved by many of Rochelle Ratner's poems.

Robert Peters
Editor, *Poets Now*

CONTENTS

1. The Sand Dune

2. Practicing To Be A Woman

3. Remnant

THE SAND DUNE

PORTRAIT

Swimming.
I'd guess I swam a hundred miles
with white fish spewing from my ankles
and blue fish dangling from my waist.
I'd look up
and see how they circled —
it made me think that great feats
lay behind me.
All the fish I'd dreamt of there forever.
The water drew a mother's heart
on dry sand, on the wet sand
left her footprints
for the chloride.
Men carried tubes of air
instead of babies
and filled their hands with spears
like ancient hunters.
I thought
there'd be something I'd give them —
a blue fish
or a white fish —
one with deep set eyes
that loved the water.

WOMAN TOSSING HER INFANT SON IN THE POOL

Mother, I sit at your side
as you hold the photograph.

Silently you ask
why I never let you take pictures,
never wanted something like this
to remember those years by.
Calmly, your fingers edge
toward an answer.

I watch your trembling hand
as if I'm watching myself
five years old
standing in the ocean
turning blue with cold
yet refusing to come out.

I can be as stubborn as you
because every once in awhile
father takes me out
past where the waves break.
And both of us sense you
on the beach behind us
crumpling that towel in your mouth
as if giving birth again.

Even now your teeth clench.
Your silence grates at me
until, year after year at camp,
I refuse to let them teach me
how to swim.

At the beach I lie on my back,
one towel rolled beneath my head
and another spread under me.
I push aside all the talk;
water's the only sound that calms me.

Gradually, I'm learning to overcome fear
and not be ashamed in a bathing suit.
Last summer I tried to learn to swim.
I'm stronger now, I can kick my legs.
Watch me.

TAUNTING

SEAWEED EATER, FLY CATCHER, WORM BITER
WHALE CHASER, WAVE MAKER, MUMMY LEGS

I'VE GOT YOUR CAP
AND YOU CAN'T GET BACK IN THE SEA
WITHOUT IT

HERE, CATCH

And they toss stones.
Sharp, brittle stones
stick in my fins.
I would like to shove them
down their throats.
I would like to throw them back
and put their eyes out.

Instead I huddle into myself
and sit there motionless
I don't know why they pick on me.

It's because I don't eat
the same things they do.
I'm smaller than they are
and my hair's too long, too knotted.
I swim better than they do
and they're jealous,
I matured before they did.
There's no way I can tuck my breasts in,
no way I can hold my breath long enough.

Someday I'll have all the powers
my mother had.
But for now I find some corner,
some hole chewed in the rock,
and crawl into it.

When they have children
I'll take them into the sea with me
and leave two large rocks
in the crib instead, in darkness.
And I won't give them back, not ever.
Meanwhile I crouch alone in their game.
I'm tired playing.

SURVIVAL

As a child she dug the tiny sand crabs up
and filled her bucket with them.
Every time the wave returned
there would be three or four in the hole she'd dug—
iridescent colors, pearl-like white, pink, yellow,
crowded together till they died
from lack of air or water.
Even so she dug them up summer after summer,
the smaller the better, she was afraid of the large crabs.
They taught her she had to fear the large ones.
If she just makes herself small
no one will fear her. So she thinks. So she wishes.
Sometimes it's all tied up in her head.
Her legs are hurting.

THE AFRICAN VIOLET
(for my father)

For the second time this week
I call in tears:

I am not your daughter
I don't know who I am
I just don't know.

This is a voice on the phone.
This is a call for which, you say,
you'll pay the charges.
It is three a.m., four a.m.

I am more wound up than the clock,
see how I'm shaking.

Why?

It is not my season.
I must learn to relax at times
and not feel so useless.

With all your love
you speak of the african violet
and its velvet leaves.

Yes, I recall — on the kitchen window,
blooming just once each year.

There's a trust it will always come back.
You can always call us.

PERSON WITH A MASK ON

I.

I tell you I'm from Atlantic City.
Then I go on to explain
that I'm from Margate,
a suburb where most
of the rich people live.

Already I've given
more of myself
than you realize.

You should visit here —
you'll understand me,
you'll know why I'm shy at times
and bold
almost arrogant
at other times.

You'll find traces of me
in alleys between buildings
or on vacant lots
where buildings were torn down.
You'll find traces in the traffic lights
at each corner.

Laughing,
I say again
'this is where I came from.'
Always past tense.
I speak as if this town and I
were separate.

II.

Look for what's missing.
You'll see the weeds
that I picked
as a child
and gave my mother

the weeds
that I kept for myself

the weeds I didn't pick
one year

because I found
a building had been built there —

the yellow brick school
we lived next door to.
It was a part of me also.

They promised my parents
when we bought
our house
they didn't have plans to build
for at least ten years.

This was four years later.
No more weeds left.

III.

Look at those waves.
Since you can't take one
and hold it in your hand
you say it's not real.

Still, we speak of the ocean
as calm today.
I speak of myself
with a headache or an earache.

You see a pigeon
rushing toward the food
I offer up.
But what if I didn't throw it,
just made motions,
my arm
reaching toward my pocket
emerging fist closed
gesturing to air?

He would still dart against me.
And the other birds
would think I'd fed him.

IV.

I speak of myself as a bird.
But you understand what I'm saying.

Bird, city, me.
The old lighthouse
now painted red
where it was blue

my grandfather's house
so large I can't remember
all the rooms,

with a third floor
that I've never even seen
(he lives alone there now
ever since his wife died)

my father's office
which he keeps expanding

the boat ride we took
around the island
and the men who begged for coins
along the boardwalk.

I show you my grandfather's house,
my father's office.
Nothing more.
I give you my hand,
bent at the wrist.

I brought you here
to show you parts of things.

We never think about landmarks.
Or if we do
we want them to be
the way that waves are.
Distorting shape and form.
Always of interest.

THE CEREMONY

So many plants have died in this house.
A single flower reminds me,
cut short, alone in its bud vase.
Without others to compare it to
it could be a bush, a tree, a forest.
Surveying the apartment, its wedding night.
Carnation, but with a slight change
it could be *coronation*.
Mother, look back on today
as if you were crowned, or born.
From the flowers you brought as an offering
this small pink flame was given back.
Thoughtlessly, you assume it will survive here.

ROCHELLE BUCKTEETH

They say she sucked her thumb so long
her two front teeth not only bucked
but parted to make room for it.
In second grade
she still doesn't smile
with her mouth closed.
She'll be sorry.
She'll have to get braces

twice — in fifth grade
she's really too young
and keeps putting her tongue
against the wires and breaking them
till the dentist gets upset
and yanks them off,
again in eighth grade
but by then she just doesn't care.
She'll have eight teeth pulled
so they can push the others back
(four the first time, four the second)
and by the time she's twenty
all her other teeth will start to rot.

SINGING LESSONS

They kept saying
I had to take singing lessons
because all we have is song
and don't *you* want to be
bewitching

They forgot to say
I had to open my mouth first,
hear the notes
not think them

But what if
some ghastly tone emerged?
Please teacher,
move back

Since I was a child
they said something's wrong
with the way you speak,
dragging me
to speech class after speech class

Didn't they realize
trying to force me
only made me fight

Didn't they know
Couldn't they see
Didn't they understand
how much one song would cost?

RENOVATION

Putting a smock on the boardwalk
that it might look its best
for those who visit.

No,
the people never do this.
Only their words are dressed,
their tight-veiled hands
that search the sand
for treasure.

This is what she wanted.
This is the beach-block
alone with the wind
from fall till summer,

the homing pigeon
in a cage the sea rolls up
to hold it.

She keeps a lamp in each window,
keeps a fire burning
for the dead son.
And her neighbors say it's wrong—

wrong to want so much,
wrong to clothe the boardwalk.

THE SAND DUNE

What is it you want me to do, Mother?
Anything I could say,
you've said it first.
You were here for nearly forty years
before me
and your shoes are two sizes too big
for me to follow.

—The same things can be done with a doll
propped on the cold sill,
lips not moving,
eyes painted to stay open always.

Black curtains covered the windows.
Not the fact so much
as what was hid behind them.
And yet the people spoke
from one face to another,
eyes like crosses
burning on a lawn.

It's not my fault,
I never knew your home.
True, we've visited Liberty Terrace—
an alley I tried to find once
by myself
          and couldn't.

Different children play in the houses now.
I've never been inside them.

What I've gotten most from you
is a taste for gambling.
Except you never gamble.
It's in the blood—
Atlantic City, every second generation.
For a week you've owed me nineteen dollars.

THE THIRD ATTRACTION

Searching for the man
at Planter's Peanuts
who shook hands with them
when they were kids

his costume
like a straw balloon
around his torso.

This new man
isn't the same:

not tall enough,
and look how that skinny suit

fits him.
Even his jet black arm
shoots out too quickly:
a boat caught in the marsh,
its oars for rudders.

Peanut shells
tossed into water
drift off slowly, floating.

TASTE

Ingredients thrown together
with nothing in common:

I want to scream
to the baker in the window
that his cakes cannot succeed
because too many people watch him.

He smiles and stirs.
He pours the mixture gently.
It took him thirty years
to learn to do that.

Slower than he,
I've spent my life relating.
Always through a showcase window
on the boardwalk
where the man who makes taffy
tries to stretch his life out,

I've been going away
for four years
and coming back once a summer
on vacation —

all the different flavors,
shapes, and colors.
Let me get the candy off my fingers.

THE CATERPILLAR RIDE

I.

Too big to hold in her hand.
Too fast to stay with.
Surely
there must be other ways
to love.

Together
as lightning on wires
all last evening.
Sound meeting sound
meeting frenzy.
And the small bird
who flew to the wire
just at dark
was there this morning
dead.

Animals grow
according to their cages:
a small cage
and the animal stays small,
give him lots of room
he'll keep on growing.
This explains
my feeling as we ride —
the awning
closing us in,
dissecting growth, our eyes in tiny cages.

We have to build our own enclosure.
But best to wait
until the land is narrow —
some road
they once started to build
and then abandoned.

Dirt piled up, dug out for us.
There must be a hundred roads like that.
Mountains on both sides
keep us within them,
even though one mountain's
made of water.

II.

updownwtartfastdownupdownfastslow
Or something like that.
It could go on
forever in that cycle
if there weren't a man there
to stop it.
Look at him sneer as we enter.
He knows
we suspect him of cheating,
giving someone else
a longer ride.
And one of these times
when there's no one else around
he'll fix us good,
keep us there so long
we won't know what we're doing.
Maybe this time.

And maybe we'll be grateful
if it is.
Easy as the entrance
to the Holland Tunnel
with the traffic going fast,
one direction only.
I drove through there
so many times
and never thought twice,
never gave a second look
to the man in the toll booth.
This much trust
not carelessly given.

III.

This ride alone
can stand for all the city:
when in motion
green and brown
merges with the ocean
and when still
not enough
to draw the children.
People who live here
find their lives are like this—

in summer
merged with the tourists,
in winter
sedated.
Everyone rides
for the hell of it,
screams
whether they intended to
or not.
Noise of the motor—
chug-a-clink-chug-a-clink-chug-a-clink-chug-
a-clink-chug-a-clink-chug-a-clink
even as a heartbeat.

This ride, both faster
and slower than the city,
encloses a city only
in its dark.
Yet how simple it is
to draw the awning tight enough
to hide us:
from floor to ceiling
one black mass.
We watch the people before us,
each the thing
which makes a city private.

The handle bar is lifted
then clamped down
and locked.
Door to the building.
At midnight
fumbling for the key.
No key to be found.
We simply
clutch the knob
then turn it gently.
Watch how many times it circles.
And the wheels beneath us
circle more.
The star-gazer says the stars
are barely moving.

How could he know?

IV.

Before the awning closes
we must wave.
Waving from the side of the track
nearest to the people.
But just for the hell
we'll wave
from the opposite side.

Not to do things
exactly as expected.
At this speed
there's such a blur
no one will know
if we waved or didn't.
So we won't wave.
Save our muscles for the fast spots
where they're needed.
Part of growing up.

A fog starts
where no land exists.
Coming off the sea each morning,
moving from Longport up
till it fills the houses.
The confusion
that sets in deep
between the pulse and fingers.
I feel my blood pressure rising.
Dizzy,
I can't even make out
stores on the boardwalk.
Some tourist *I* am!

V.

One more bridge between
the self and others,
giving some false excitement.
A faint glow is felt through the cover.
So faint
the cat
runs back into the corner.
This attempt to feed herself
was all for nothing.
And leaving
the child leaves his jacket
on the seat,
comes forth crying
that he was cold
with nothing to hang onto.
The dark not resistant enough.

I ride in silence.
You won't catch me
laughing and screaming.
I have better things to do.
The cat walks on my desk
as I write this:
even she
walks freely
not strapped in the seat
no purr emitting from her body.

Between the metal wheels and I:
no communication.

Plans don't always work out.
I have to live with the screams
of all the others.
Someone murdered.
Living with myself
before and after.
I find myself
shivering
clinging to the side,
my teeth well-parted
with a desperate sound between them.
I spoke after all.
I couldn't bear the silence.
The silence of beds at night
when no one's in them.

I wanted to make this a sex poem.
But where there are tourists
there is no real sex.
Doormen at hotels
and rides like this one.
Silent.
My body sunk in cushions.
At sea, I guess
you'd always feel such motion.
On top of the water now,
coming up for air, then more air.

VI.

The last ride was the best
I've ever had —
my head was thrown back
to the man behind me.
So fast I lost my breath,
the screams continued
from another body.
I have one set of hands on the bar
but another set won't dare
come near it.
They hang limply at my stomach.
A feeling of being myself
and not myself,
for once so complete
the worlds outside me quiet down.
My foot jams against the floor.
The floor contains it.
No one speaks
until the drugs start working,
no one questions
what another's wishing.
United
as eggs in a nest
have never dreamed of,
and set to hatch
if one just says the right word
very loudly.

Something breaking open.
No longer any fear or doubt
inside me.
You on that end of the seat
and I on this end.
Nothing in the center.
Just empty space
that both of us can fall toward.
But really, the sea's in the center.
The sea
and the beach
are everywhere around us.
There's no such thing as *empty*.
Even so you cling to that rail,
I to this one.
Good kids.

A marble on the tracks
would be disaster.
But two marbles,
three?
They'd counteract each other.
Glossy colors,
visible in darkness.
No getting off
at such a speed,
with such a pressure.
Gravity's one thing
eggs are still unsure of.
It's certain they balance, in spite of it.

EVENING WITH THE GUEST
(the rooming house)

All right. A dentist from Raleigh.
Tell of the hillsides
and mountains.
Though anything but the sea
seems out of place here.
Every now and then
a stranger,
but most winters
no one comes
and no one leaves.
When you speak of home
you must shout to get
above the roar
of ocean.
The boardwalk's railed off
from the gulls
for you.
Talk from that distance.

BEST OF LIFE APARTMENTS

I sit out front for hours.
Everyone I meet

tells me his story,
how he started for some other town
and wound up here:

poverty so great
they made this a tourist resort.
All the rich people came.
It worked so well
they even believed it themselves.

They line these benches.
Week
after week
sitting calmly,
their legs spread out for sex
which has outgrown them.

Alone at night,
a man jerks up in bed.
That dream again.
He flicks the lamp on.
He touches all ten fingers.
He calls to his mistress
(doubling as a night nurse)
for her to come and shut the light out,
try to fool him.

From THE LULLABIES

Fog, Sara.

That's the best I can say about this morning.
It makes the ocean vast
and majestic
when the water comes right to my feet
before I see it.
There's something proud and cruel,
if this is heaven.

Just an hour later.
I sit on hard sand
close to where the waves end.
Low tide
yet the rocks are covered.

Groups of herons
sleep on the beach behind me.
The largest and quietest birds I've ever seen here.
Wonderful grey markings

(nothing's pure white).

I've written your name in the sand.
It should last for a little while, anyway.

As I sit here sun breaks through the clouds,
slowly and politely.

In New York your funeral service
must be starting.
I can see them now —
your sisters in their places.
　　　DAMN IT! I should be there with them.

Death is something the waves understand,
Sara. Please believe me.
As tribute to you
the sun is in again.
Fog dips and covers.
I don't want to take off my shoes, haven't touched
　　　　　　　　　　　　　　　　the water.

8/15/73
Atlantic City

*

ATLANTIC CITY TO NEW YORK.
It's not that far.
Today, coming back on the bus,
I talked the whole time.

35

Manhattan's been your home
these fourteen years.
For you it was further than for me.

The city's not a place to be alone.
Mugged six years ago,
your hip broken, in the same hospital.
That was the beginning.

A person doesn't have to die
to be so quiet.
There's many different ways
we talk while living.
Like a record, we rotate toward the center,

toward the part in each of us
where we know already
how to listen.
The past few days, it's easier to see that.

I spoke with the rabbi awhile,
standing at your grave.
He wasn't as calm as I hoped he'd be.

Last night I sat in the church
but couldn't think straight.
Still, I felt close to what was real in you.

You must understand,
the church was an outward form, only.

8/16/73
New York

*

Today was the first time in months
I heard the church bells.

          But I know they require more than that.
What was I supposed to do?
I'm not a Catholic.
I couldn't have gone to the Mass
and sat back believing.
What I want from a God is within me.

    Birth and death,
like the retina of my eye
as the mirror sees it.
I feel both absorbed in my days now—
Sara's death
and the things it bore in me.
          Not an infant, exactly

or else, yes,
some new life I must take care of.
        Helpless, crying, pleading to know what this is.

That hunger which tears, alone, nourish.
There's a doll I had as a child
                which really cried.

    I lay her down
                and squeezed water into her mouth.
                That's what the trick was.

8/19/73
New York

*

    Often, a place in the crowd . . .

Easy in the city.
   Sunlight behind me, the baseball field in front.
30,000 people!
There's something which draws us together here,
                the pennants and the food,
                the struggling faces.

Losing myself.
I can begin again now.
   A tiredness, something like joy,
               creeps all around me.

The ball is white and round
                  with small black stitches.
            It has no beginning nor ending.
            The players,
                  some of them younger than I am,

must perform here.
A game of personalities, mainly —
      our names fading in their names.

Nothing's given up
if looked at that way.
We're PUSHING, STEALING, SCREAMING,

frantic to make time move quickly.
      The batter HITS, RUNS, SLIDES into a fielder.
They could be you and me. Any two veiled people.

8/20/73
New York

A CORNER WINDOW
ON THE BEACH SIDE

I.

our neighbor shot the eagle
and he's scared.
we really don't see many eagles here.
he knows we'll get him.
yeah.

"i didn't mean to kill her.
i aimed at the hawk
that was near her
and i only missed.
i only
had one chance."

he'll pay.
he's sure he'll pay.
we throw stones at him
cause we like to.

II.

i don't want to tease you
or stand by your bed
say it's not true

you're getting better
take it slow

i don't want to touch you
take your hand you
reach out to me
yes and i feel crazy
dry with thirst, my own thirst
only healthy

i don't want to watch you
see your pain
you rise in bed
fall back
the covers rise before you
shrieking, looking out
toward me

i don't want you to ask me
you might sense my guilt
or watch me crying there
the one who never cries

i don't want you to guess
and so i told a boy
last night
that i would love him
if he'd let me stay
i'd never have to face you.

III.

the empty bed
ruffled
gone

i search for you
later

"death was peaceful
she   didn't seem to
know"

(your room's cold
the curtains   almost wake me)

the nurse
says that you called me
"rhoda,
rhoda . . ."

not rochelle.

IV.

those moonrocks really rotate.

i tried to hold you.

that moon might leave its axis.

twine you in stars.

then light shines too bold
to look up and
the moon gives in before
we feel it grow.

the moon has seven wives.

i took your hand.

a child the moon
which keeps us there when
other moons have quit.

PRACTICING TO BE A WOMAN

REHEARSAL

The fish tail's only painted on.
She's pretending to be a mermaid
but actually she folds her legs
beneath her,
half kneeling, half balancing
on her knees.

She's been sitting there
long enough to feel the muscles
harden into bones —
to move now would be dangerous.

The point is she's trapped there
and the walls of the trap
are closing in.
She doesn't want to be
like the people around her
and nobody's bothered to tell her
there are other people.
She'll never learn unless she moves
and won't move until she has to.

Sometimes she wakes from sleep
and tries to get away,
but her legs are so frail by now
she falls down.
Sometimes in the morning people tell her
and she doesn't remember falling.
It's no good to remember.

PRACTICING TO BE A WOMAN

1.

Not that sort of woman,
sticking her little finger out
to be dainty

the ones I'm attracted to
have more sensible things to do

like putting effort
into being friends with women.
Not all of them

but one woman:
me.

It was natural
when she was giving a party
to invite me

but the room wasn't small enough
for all those people.

2.

What does it mean to love?
Each clings to the woman
she's come with, as if
afraid she'll leave

a smile might crack a face
or lighten a voice
they try so hard to deepen.

My friend caters to each couple in turn:
they kiss her on the mouth,
hug her in friendship
but don't touch skin to skin.

Wait a minute,
they always told me love expands.
I sense your bodies growing tighter.

If you don't enjoy yourselves
why bother?

I want to know why
when men love men
they seem to have so much fun
yet when women love women
they become so solemn.

3.

Mother, you protected
and played with me
so I had no need
for other friends.
That isolated, how could I help
but become self-centered?

Each day I'm getting more
like the fourth wife grandpa chose
because she had no children

it never seemed right
to call her grandma
though I know
it was hard for her —

year after year
grandpa sold beach chairs,
lugging the comfort toward the sea
for other women
while she waited on the beach
with iced tea for him.

I played in the sand
but watched them and learned
how a woman becomes selfish
yet loves.

THE CAPTIVE

I am caught in the act
of being female:

here I am

head cocked sideways,
trying hard to smile.
(To some this comes as naturally
as loving.)

I draw my tongue up to my lip
and move it slowly.
I relax my muscles,
let my arms dangle a bit
to show my breasts off.

My thoughts find a spot in air
and try to mend it.

APPEASEMENT

When a woman trembles
it means nothing

when her body shakes all over
she is simply walking

back and forth
the stars reflected in the river,
she is one star
only

and though water moves on top of her
she trembles.

I am not that woman
though I see her
bending down

like this I still myself
and I am nothing
to the movement that surrounds me.

THE TIGHTROPE WALKER

Thin and graceful,
sure of every step

won't look down
but forward

with the wire swaying

juggled each time a thought
is added to it.

She is the child in me
that no one speaks of

and I among the thousands
cheering her.
Pray the stunt will be over.

. . .

After years of study
she's alone

the spectators
too far away —

delusions

as on a journey
heading toward the mountains
she sees forms emerge
and then vanish.

It's simply the leap
from a far peak
to a near one.

. . .

The net beneath her
like some phallic form

offers this much assurance:

slipping
she will find herself
within it

a lover
confused by her presence

to whom she lends only her body.

She gives
and then reclaims that which is given

knows a person merely
by his smile

surface
colored by wind and rain
past recognition.
Still she keeps one hand extended.

THE CAT

The cat won't play today.
Her eyes reflect me.

In her
I can sense what you wanted:
one warm thing
to cuddle up against you.

This morning
cold, the heat on for a moment.
Half awake, we hear the pipes knock
as if to give us warning
bring us back there
one more winter.

Like a man in a mask
wind walks the rooftops.
For now it has clouds to tend to.

Write only:
some days are clearer than others.

AN ACCOUNT OF THE STRUGGLE
(for Jan)

This is not me speaking

or
the part that talks
is no poet

I can't be two places at once
must save, must
separate.

Still that doesn't solve the problem:
what can we say
to begin?
Between poets it's simple

we say nothing, look
past the words to words.
We have read
(or pretend to have read)
each other's work
and have that to start from

besides
what I want to show is the poet
not the woman
yet you can get me to sway
between the two.

No wonder you find it so hard sometimes,
with everyone fighting against that.

SOME NIGHTS

Some nights I sit in the bathtub
and think how one thing lovers do
is take baths together.

The cold white sides close in on me
till I notice that under water
my fingers are short and fat
while my legs stretch smoothly
as I guess his cock would.

My thighs drift apart naturally.
When my stomach's cramped
the water eases it.
The nipples of my breasts
seem to rise and float
as I lie back.

I jiggle the faucets,
first too hot then too cold;
will I never get it right?
It's no longer something I can control.

Some nights my body seems so weightless
that I think perhaps here, perhaps someday.

BIG FLOPPY FISH IN A PUDDLE

A few years ago we had to choose:
to be a minnow in a big pond
or a big floppy fish in a puddle.
We forgot nature takes care of that,
determining the size of each fish
by how much room there is.

Fat thing squatting like a frog
on that tiny rock,
your hair seems blonde now
but the minute you get it wet
green, slimy roots show.

You boast of how no man
can resist your song.
I know those men —
they were your friends once
and they've still too much respect
to run out on you.

Even your six year old daughter
sits with her land-locked father
stuffing sand in her ears to shut you out.
You wouldn't dare let the rhythms of the sea
come through.

Will you blush if I say how insecure you are?
All those drunk nights
seven or eight years ago
we lay together on the bottom, looking up.
We wanted the same things then.

I came today out of friendship
to hear songs I once thought were good
distorted, sung too loudly,
the words muffled through your smile
while you bang shells together
and call that music.

But you can't drown me out
any more than the waves can.
And secretly you know I don't enjoy this,
why I won't even lean off my rock
and sway to your song
for fear you'd push me under.
That's the kind of friend you are.

But just once, for just a moment,
leave off combing that straggly hair,
turn and look at me, I'm singing for you.

MY BODY'S WHAT THE WAVES
COULD NOT REMEMBER

My body's what the waves could not remember.
Tonight the sea's too much a child
to write here.

Instead I watch lights through my window,
cars that stop and start
like buddhas.

I'll say
that men inside them are my lovers:
thin and blonde, or short

with deep black eyebrows.
They collect the trash
along the sidewalk—

it's a fat man walking backwards
or a frog with broken throat
who swims where land swims.

A BABY'S FINGER

A baby's finger walks inside your head. I hadn't
realized it would move so slowly, or that it would have
been so far away. And look, you've grown mold on your
forehead. It's as if you'd put on hair, but grey already.

I stare at you, an old woman today. Looking into
your skull I see landscapes, gently turning: little girl
who rolls down the hill, to find at the bottom, dust.
Like her, will you get up, dry yourself off in sunlight,
the glow that you're holding, within?

No, you're more the earth's ray. You spring back,
mad, your light piercing. You want to fight those who
forgot you. You want to leap from the table and, ghost-
like, fly round the room, toward walls and fixtures.

DEFINITION, AFTER A FOLKSONG

I see myself, at times, as a flower
with a hundred petals of corn
unsheathed to sunlight.
It's important you know
I didn't have to be this,
I had the choice once.
I could have been
top half fish
bottom half human.
But I'd seen mothers
nursing their young
and wanted that most of all.
When my breasts grew hard
then popped forth
then fattened
I felt as if the world
was inside me.
I didn't know my stomach
left him no room to get in,
no place for his magic child
to stem from.

THE LITTLE SEA MAID

1. (Maturity)

The most important part
about being a woman
is that every month
the blood comes.
But of course I knew
I could never be that,
so the kind witch
in giving me feet
made the blood pour from them.
I loved him so much
I gladly bore the pain
as I followed him everywhere
bleeding, bearing child after child
where I left my footprints.

2. (Letting My Eyes Speak)

Twenty slaves sing to my prince
each day at sunset
while I sit on a cushion
by his side, his right side.
Their voices are on key at least
but once I sang
better than all of them.

With my deep blue eyes
I try to tell him
how I told the witch
I would give anything she asked.
How, when she cut out my tongue,
I thought I'd lost everything.
But whatever made me think
he'd believe my stories?
He loves me
as one loves a little girl,
as he loved that temple maid
who saved his life
when once the sea washed him,
by chance, to the temple courtyard.
My lover doesn't understand —
I was the one who brought him there.
I, a white sea-maid he thought
was foam on the water.

3. (Surfaces)

Foam on the water.
It scares me half to death.
Had I stayed beneath the sea
tending my garden
with its little marble sailor
in three hundred years
I would have become foam,

not even a grave
to mark that I existed.
Now there is hope:
if the prince loves me so much
he forgets father and mother
I will gain a human soul.
But if he should marry another
I will be foam the next day.

4. (A Chorus of Sisters)

Sister, youngest sister,
cast your beautiful eyes here.
See, tonight something is different.
Just as you went to the witch
with your golden tongue
now we have gone to her
with hair like roses.
Our curls swirl beside us
in the churning tide
because our grandmother's hair
falls out with worry.
We gave it to the witch for you.
Then from the longest locks
she made this knife.
Reach out, take it quickly,
it is sharp, do not cut yourself.

Stab it in the prince's breast
while his new wife
lays her head there
and forever return home.
Sister, you can still be one of us.

HOWLING AT THE MOON
(for P.S.)

As long as he's in my arms
I'll do as I please
and he won't dare go back,
he's afraid of you.

That's the difference between us:
while you hold your body
out as a wall
to block his leaving
I softly walk my fingers
down from mind to heart.

If he doesn't let me down
I take him down,
down till we're out of your sight.
Then he tells me he misses you.

What are you waiting for?
Others would have fingered knives
long before this.
You've no comb, no mirror,
nothing to battle with.
Anyway, I promised him I'd try.
I sink lower in the water,
slowly curve the tip of my tail
for poise and balance,
pat down my gills
as others smooth their skirts.

I know he'll come to me.
They always do.
But the other women
never seemed to mind,
they found me harmless,
a dead sponge on the surface.

He'll come to me.
I'll toss him about in my arms,
let his head bob above the water
just to tease you.
Stupid, jealous bitch.
There was a time I came to *you*
as friend.

THE LAMB

You're the lamb who sheds his fur
to be the king's son.

The wind's at your back tonight
colder.
More intense, you cry.

I hadn't noticed.

Your shaved head's lost its warmth.
You say you're lonely.
You tell me
your father ran out on you.
Left you on a hill too steep for travel.

DRIVING

Tonight you give coins to a blindman.

I sit back
want the eyes stuck in my breasts
to find your shelter:

for once
you give so easily.
So darkly.

   Beneath the car
the street rolls back our echo. The leather's
stiff
and doesn't bend to fit me.
Home at last —

a place where rocks are ground down.
Nothing begs here.

COLD & NO CABS ON FIRST AVENUE

I visit him
laughing, a child almost,
playing a game

No.
It wasn't a game
or if it was
I wasn't playing

The walls around us
too far apart. There's
so much room here.
Really.
I wanted him close.

So.
It's late,
I'll be leaving. Nothing more.

Then. A final effort.
Sign the book?
Hidden, now its cover
in my hands
pale blue.

He took it
wrote my name 'with love'
said he couldn't think
what else to say.

LOVE POEM

He cuddles, he cherishes.
I can't begin to say
how good it feels.

He smooths palms over my back
presses my breasts against him.
In return I promise
never to resist.

But in love I saw myself
and saw the future

an old woman
with no child to tend
or to tend me.

Against my will
I saw that I fit his body
as I lay there half asleep,
praying not to be mortal.

POEM OF THE DRESS

At first it was agreed
he'd do the cooking.
And I tested him:
I refused his unbaked bread
and his well-done bread

I refused to go with him
till its crust was crisp, thinner
than the finest oyster shells,
soft and moist inside
like all things at sea are.

But within a month
he was pulling my hair
to whip me into line.
I cooked
and ate the crumbs he threw me,
or his voice made it seem that way.

I began to hate myself,
hate cooking and cleaning,
everything feminine,
even water only emerged
from hard metal hooks, upside down,
which sent chills through my spine
every time I touched them.
I refused to wash.

Day and night I lay in bed,
in pain, and mornings I spit up food
as if I was seasick;
I was afraid
to put my food down hard on land
and the fear was killing me,
my own childhood pounding in my chest
like a fish swallowed whole.

THE WELCOME
(for Bob)

Like a clock placed
in a kitten's bedding

at your house I find
I've wanted more than this

your touch as the final proof
there are two kinds of loneliness.

YOU'RE ASLEEP

You're asleep in the next room
and sleep's your mistress.

You breathe
and the walls cling tighter,

they rush to see the child
who's born between us

(we were made as whales
and mated freely).

We love, embrace, and kiss
without quite meeting.

We give ourselves fears
which the sea had.

WE PRETEND TO MAKE LOVE

We pretend to make love as the rain falls.
Crying that you're warm
you press against me

and my body moves
to be the air around us.
I've got to keep you cool and close

to help me.
I've forgotten so much that it hurts you
yet I've kept the bed unmade—

the words that we're speaking grow softer,
tongues that touch a moment
then curl back. One kind of rainbow.

SWANSONG

Sleep, my child, sleep
for it was in some trance
I gave birth to you.
Your father's arms were cold
his bed was strange
but still he calmed me
into lying there.

Sleep, my little girl,
the night is so dark
it can seem endless.

When you wake
I will be gone from here.
Cross your legs for a moment,
pretend they're a fish tail:
be like me, my daughter.

Every single time
you smile at your father
he will see me there
in your giant eyes,
in the way your mouth curves.
When you start to cry
I will be your tears —
little by little I'll come back
to check on you.

Late at night, each night
I've prayed I could stay
and take care of you.
But it no longer matters
for the tide is in,
the waves are stormy.
Someday, I thought,
I'd take my family there,
your father at my side
proud of me,
you bundled in my arms
showing the world it was possible.
Your mother has been dreaming.
But now sleep tight, sleep my child.

YOU FIND ME IN THE SLEIGH

You find me in the sleigh
wrapped all in velvet:

going somewhere warm today
where heat makes snow a toy
and ground a playpen.

A short time I lie back
and let the winds roar
till the hills get rough
and I get anxious—

I stare out through the blades
at white around me.
Snow gives more than I can.

ON THE BACK OF MY RIGHT HAND

On the back of my right hand
I build a city,

place tiny trees and houses
with streets that go up straight,

come down in circles.
I gently wave my arm

as if to show you —
the glow between us

drifts a bit, then settles.
I've built a town to lose things

yet find myself in sun
that comes through fingers.

RELEASED

Anything, any wish you choose
or all your wishes,
I will grant them the second
you take your hook out of my neck.
I have all the powers
of creatures I have brought low
in my watery home —
I can cast spells,
walk on air, heal the injured.
Muckle gude I wid you gie.

Skipper, pity this poor lass.
You already have the food
for ten family dinners,

while I am only partly edible
and might not cook up well.
Think what your wife would say
if you came home with my breasts.
Empty those buckets of yours,
count six trout, eleven flounder.
And mair I wid ye wish.

Please let me dive in again.
It's hot up here,
sun makes me lose my senses.
I want a cool rock to lie on
while the waves lull me to sleep.
Only do not follow, I beg
do not watch where I go
or chart my path.
There's muckle evil in the sea.

You need not be frightened.
If you let me go I will teach
that you already hold wishes
in your large, sweaty palms.
Instead of keeping watch on me
step back and look around.
Sailor, tailor, take your knife in hand.
Scoom weel your fish, look inside yourself.
Skipper, *scoom weel your fish.*

REMNANT

THE GEESE PURRING

The geese purring, near sleep, before turning their
heads —

You begin, a threat to the distance.
But not eyes, not leaves, not windmills
will hinder your pattern,
your mountain.
You contain the remembrance of woman
as stars contain night.
                    The sky
is a ghost of its very thunder,
where the flight of the homing-bird
howls
in silence —
the stillness, no less still than you.

Having approached you quickly,
from behind,
the clouds have won, their fur stiffens.

The black discs press their thighs
against your breast,
whether you stir or are resting.

No takers.
Night after night the wings flicker,
grow heavy and fade, without calling.
Mask. Willow not pregnant nor warm
in the grass where you hide.
You wake here, a casual flower

observing no change

but with the next seed beating at your lips,
desperate for sound, enclosing sound . . .

. . . to be a woman's necklace

clasping, held onto
by secret strings, in the evening,
when the flight is of hands and thoughts, preparing.

THE HELL DOLL

I.

The pregnant bird
turned loose
in a female sky . . .

one wing flapping, turning shyly,
persuasively over the next, steady
falling
tumbling
twisting the clouds
into speech. It was
like his hands, now, at the table,
shoveling in and out of themselves
until he can no longer
stand the pressure of her breath.

He sits beside her, an aborted stick.
This was how houses were built, perhaps—
the bricks there so long that they were fixtures,
other things
being forced to take shape around them,
give form to the dirt.

And she—
it was she who had placed him there,
opened the cage to give him his freedom,

give him his hell. He regretted
he'd not met her sooner, not been her wife.
Perhaps the child in himself would be her son.

II.

On the day of his birth
he bears his second child.
She tears at his womb, arms
groping blindly forth
like a stone in the water. They almost touch.

A clown who is also a juggler;
his hands pound the wood —
the womb splits, a shattered mirror.

Shapes ridicule themselves like a portrait,
the colors flaring, unnamed.
Two men cannot meet in the darkness.

III.

She is a lute-girl
beckoned to play for him.
She crouches on the narrow floor,
on a blanket perhaps.

Her thin arms
reach tenderly across the strings,
as across his chest.
She would sit there hour on hour,
playing one tune so softly
it seemed she could fly.

Entering the room,
a man might remark on her beauty,
her destined repose. His breath
might flutter slightly
as her voice pierced him, steady.

From her mother's arms
she'd learned music,
the gentle rhythm of her heartbeats,
her lips swaying back and forth,
enclosing his.

A man might call them lovers, nothing more.

IV.

Her body is a long dark lake
flowing into itself.
He watches always from a distance,
a ship approaching a meadow in the fog.

As day brightens,
he begins to notice tall grass
he mistook for water.

He thinks himself the echo approaching storm.
He will protect her,
cover her,
press her skin against his own,
thus changing places.

It is in much this manner
that he will approach his birth
from the other side.
He will watch his stomach swell
into her being, feel his muscles
tighten, the skin stiff,
long unused.

V.

The Roman emperors were given
shields to be held at their waists.
The bulging metal before them,
they fought for their lives.
In later days
engravings
were printed on gold —

pictures of cavalry,
duels,
scenes that said 'man'.

He is his private boyhood.
His body sprawls on a bed
in darkest night, alone, itself,
with no one
to term it male.
The sound of his blood travels
through him like a battle,
safe, unshod.

VI.

He had seen his mother
naked in the tub.
Her giant breasts hung down, much like his own.

VII.

She is given to picking berries.
She holds them in her hands
and lets them fall.
The tin balls stay
like a man in her throat.

Their soft juice becomes her mother,
tender lips
that have been stolen from his arms.

VIII.

Who
has created the idol?
Who has made the plastic doll?

Her flesh is warmed by the fire.
As wax melts it takes on new forms,
becomes a guest.
He would press it against his stomach,
molding it
as she had molded him.
And thus they would worship together, she alone.

PREGNANCY

Then the clock was awkward. And her climb
to the brown sky hardened.
                        Breathing
viewed as a recurrence of the stain, as

the gripping arm
falls over pillows. Later on she found him,

a crumbling of low briars
which his fists struck upon, which seemed
as she pushed forward

to be sinking. At every
blistered tick and frenzied echo:
   the jingling, cold sequins of blood,

tired.

   She learned only that all her children
crawled between a name they had written out.

Her breast, it seemed,
which in this flame he entered,

grew too hot.
And she realized he had planned this:
                       he was dead.

A blanket
hid them both, having fled

together, as a vine.

CONSERVATION

I.

I sculpture my brood with my mouth,
produce a formless foetus,
giving birth to ashes
or a bit of pulp.

By licking, I change the stumps
into arms and legs that clutch me
far too soon.

II.

They promise that my litter
will come in threes.

III.

Modest,
we've learned to copulate
back to back.
We wear our genitals backwards,
find it's best to look
the other way.

To conceive
we go eastward toward paradise.
I eat of the tree —
mandragora —
then feed some to him.
When we lap it up
it seduces us
and I can feel life stirring in my womb.

IV.

I throw myself on the ground
and pretend not to breathe.
I roll in red mud like a carpet
so he thinks that I'm covered with blood.

A white bird comes down
and will sit on me. She supposes I'm dead
or her egg.

POEM BEGINNING "A WARM NIGHT"

A warm night / a warm week
counting from star
           to star
              to star,
calling them mirrors or only reflectors—
these shapes in the dense
or spayed forests.
               We say that the fox
does not reason; even his fur stirs in tribute.
He knows to lead the dogs,
but not as we do.
When eggs fry it's better to hide
in the brush near a narrow slope;
better than running, or scheming,
less tiring
to be high on a neck he could watch them,
the black spots and claws.

   Five trees,
tall ones sensing twenty hammers—
even now we have recalled
the thrill of adding. Even as rain
on the leaves removes our shadows
or a fork is lifted.

So the river, guest,
is behind you. And then fifty icings
of weed. One would think to drink with you,
wander like you on the ledges.

SPRING RECESS

I.

She sleeps hearing puddles.
The branch of an oak is not seen in this storm.
Leaves, as they fly backwards, feel
the flames reaching down.
The grey nuts drift to a hollow stalk.

Like a cloudburst filling green balloons,
feel the light falling off you.
    The glass we breathe away from
is refracted in our hands.

Pebbles burst at the windmill;
a tulip combs its eyes in the mirror.
We give her plums but they turn to raisins,
flicking shadows we no longer step on.
The statues are wet, like the asphalt.

II.

Red trees.
The clapping sticks of familiar reappraisal
are stolen from magnitude
and reflected in the shy lake
Motionless phonetic parents
sway back and forth on the ground.

The farmhouse defines what is vision
as women walk along the slow road,
each cloud returned to the issuing skyline
Pink to green to silver
                    and then back

The yellow brush remains blameless
A wheel turns with
and not against your breath.

III.

You find so many tall bushes along the mountains
Voices of living valleys appear in the distance
Shadows almost fold with the warm blankets
Large plants appearing in the moon
Millions of sentimental wings hiding grass or tall
    weeds . . .

The landscape returns to where you dreamt it
There are some first leaves with a tint of completed hues
There are some imaginatively-lifted sundials
Now and then in the morning a small cat cries and his
image can be seen in the east

Yesterday I sank a steamship to the bottom of the sea
Still the same waves of tired gulls
The Egyptian mistress uncovers some humming-birds
Everyone is wearing green make-up
We go up to the top of the lighthouse
For us it's the first remembrance of ships lost in storms.

The temperature changes
Our attire is childish skirts and a white lace blouse
Secrets are important for the baggage we have hidden
In the evening we simply put aprons over our skirts
Skiffs brush us with their sails.

IV.

Wagons under streetlights carry sweaters held to skin;
this evening there will be a quarter moon.
In the darkness,
in the bronze that's drifting toward us
the petals of a weed have distant thoughts.

The stranger turns to speak to us
with the frailness of his breathing reaching out
on the asphalt, seeming cousinly and warm.
A sea laps up the many pebbles
of beaches while a wing folds in the clouds.

Someone has been pausing at the window—
it is a feeling we have always known . . .
while we listen you press your hands against the
    humming
as the seed against the lisping soil.

V.

Blue kite using the orange sky
and as usual the clouds are too strong for sunlight
so if the string falls
jackets unbutton and wait for us.
You are walking slowly now
Trucks toss some hot foam into my fingers
where I can feel the cool waters.

The wind hunching into my sight
low in these valleys
like a farmer.
Trucks rolled forward
like a road near a thunderstorm
and your leaves mounted to the clouds
as if they were postcards withered by dust.

I don't really know about fishing-boats.
Once I sat on a bicycle
far away from the wheels of a river
and was never awakened.
Leaves brushed against me and continued on
I was happy then but now
a branch has fallen across the careful string.

VI.

A mask of cushions in the April noon
I stood alone
And heard the sun fall across the courtyard
Like a broken oboe.
Close by me the windows flowed northward
With cold orange lips like a swan.

Like a chameleon my eyes have opened
In fragrant marsh
And shuffling through my footsteps
Purple leaves beat and cling.

The pine needle
Falls from my back like a storm cloud
Gathers dampness to its ridges
And the burnt arms
Drift beneath it.

VII.

This wind cannot keep blowing,
it ceases—
     A unison.

The thick chest of a river
recoils in my path. I wait, I
notice the quick lights of memories
moving north. Complacency troubles the shore.

When the sun sets I sail to the tropics.
All the natives in their gay skirts,
all the husbands rejecting deadlines
in my eyes. If only there were not this resentment
that the waves walk before us.

I wait, my mouth
waters itself at the thinking.
Tomorrow the women travel from their homes.
The door of my cabin is rocking—
A careful shape, a leaf, moves across the sea.

VIII.

Faces
eyes untouched
meticulous zircons cold now
a calm feather on a calm leaf
sees us,
    I hear a stone

I hear a corner of the river
a plant stroking air

Laughing, I hear
a houseboat and the children
pressing back, I

hear pebbles on their fingers
the lips of berries fall
the clasp of water nourishing.

IX.

That the woman
grey as half-open windows
should pause by the river this evening
and unfold her necklace
like the breeze reluctant
above a stone no bird has injured.
an orange stone possibly.

The most tender birthday
begins fairly close to a forest . . .
excited lobsters move on cardboard walls.
She would curl like a seagull in rain-clouds
but she hasn't been told about wetness.
her hands bend in steam.

Once again I sit on a tree stump
allowing moss to make me thirsty until
like a spider I thrust these pebbles
into the snow of consistency.
Wood becomes black near the sand dunes.

IN THE CAT'S DREAM, I WAKEN

1.

near the pillow
near fur

"mother"
flea   fierce roaring chain

stroke; warm
hands; quiet purring.
   untouched water.
   a fear in the paw.

2.

We were beneath a picket fence tied with
      plastic vines, with thorns pounding,
      with limbs placed on wire carts.

It was painted with symbols from Indian
      tribes in the south. Crouched   -
      between rakings of stems

The men of those fossil mountains, at
     evening, calling on gods of a
     different tongue,

Were dotting their eyelids
     with wood.

3.

dried fish   at the seacoast
bundled in string for the journey

catnip leather toy on the rug in the night

white friendly
child . . . thrown and spawned . . . toward the hurried
     bed

     her muffled breathing.

REMNANT

I.

The sense of her lying there calms me:

> a lemon rind
> a stone
> a papier-mâché doll

> getting set to have a ribbon
> tied in its hair.

> I keep my eyes focused on the black velvet
> that lines the lid of the coffin. It keeps
> threatening to fall on her, close her again
> from my sight.

It's as if she were counting backwards from twelve to
one.

> Her breath seems to flow
> like the water in a frozen stream.

> Beneath the ice are tiny fossils,
> held in place by the fins
> that brush against them   back and forth.

The trout can swim briskly in water,
alone with the waiting surface of the snow.
His colors shine frantically,
frantically

my gift.

At night there are stars in the meadow.

I watch their points swivel, take aim.

Tonight I pick one star
to call my own. It is not
the brightest   nor is it dull.   It is
an average star on an average
night.

I pretend to be a grasshopper lost in the field. My small
body
hunches, crackles

& then jumps. I pounce on the weeds,
on the shadows, on all
that moves or threatens me with life.

Everything dark bends beneath
            me.
I rise
    & I rise.

In the grass I am proud
of my body, its simple lines   Everything
                    seems so calm here. All is well.

We travel.
We bounce back and forth across cities
                    like popping men.

    We crouch in our separate boxes, covered with
        stars.
    When we wake the music shimmies

    & we bob round.

    I think of the black-leaved flower
    she wears on her dress. Its odor fills the room
    like broken glass, as if death were hurried,
        prodded,
    propped up on rags.

Here there are too many farmers, too many
lonely men who wish to farm.

The thick topsoil
weighs down their hands
with its fraudulent green.

I sprawl on the velvet
                    (sheltered)
        my head in her lap.

        Her fingers are chilling,
        remorseful. I press against them,
        a tightrope.

A body grown thin.

Her eyes are like crickets in daylight.

        They dive meekly
        in her skull
        & won't peer out.

I hunt for them,
awkward,
escaping,
curled into balls of themselves,
a borrowed cat.

Their haunted wings razor my elbows,
demented guide.

I feel her ghost at play in the woods
where the coon left a path.
I become that ghost,
that whiteness
becomes my shield.
I flap across mourners.
delighted. I am best.
I am first child.

I am bonded nest in her stomach. I pound and I plea.

I tell her there were others, but I lie.

II.

In my rage I am given a Monday.

A candle burns above her
& drips on her chest.   Its wax forms shapes
                                            forms children
                                            forms a truce.

      It tickles her compact smile
      & she laughs just for me.

I can feel her beckoning toward me
            & almost leave. But her
            shrouded breasts stop me. Wait.
                              You begin too soon.
                              You
                  must be patient. A sea.

      A white bird
      sheds its feathers
      on the beach.
            As the wind rises,
            sand builds in tiny drifts
            about their guise.

It seems to cradle them,
                        softly.

Under the waves there are flowers. Treacherous vines.

    Their stems tear across my feet & my ankles grow
        weak.
    They chain me; I cannot leave to meet
    the rising tide.

        In the tents of shepherds
        she is a sheep. I
    let her skip over the hills
    or run wild in the field.

    Out of charity I cling to her,
    permit her to enter my fruit
    so I waken in fear.

    She catches birds in her absence,
        tosses them, sweet on her tongue.
    Her shadow is a blurry lantern, resembling hate.
    Her heard bones defer me, explode.
                        Like air,
                        I am carried across her —

a gangster.
a wife.

A plane voids the distance between us.

    She calls to the Jew
    like a savior,

    draws a fiddle
    from his ashen hair.

We strike up a dance in the darkness, vipers of smoke.

    A nail twists loose from the coffin,
    is placed on the blue-flowered river:

            caraway eye.

    I ride on her face like a fire,
    hang myself from her palate,
    as if a blank snake.

Wasps curl about her face,
swinging in tiny clusters
on the pulse of her breath.

Their glass bodies flutter upward,
        rusting in explanations,
        desperate in groves.

    She is a youngster. Simple.
    A trapped embryo.

    Day after day I accept her,
           a gentle return.

She is a paranoid archway,
      an axis of walls,
       a meadow of amulets tied in their primitive myths.

She coils around rivers:
      an owl's shift, birth of prey. With the abbots
      she wakens, forces the moon to her side
& is open in love. I make her into a lampshade,

    a naked child.

QUARRY

THE HUNTING SONG

Stillborn, we know it's joy
to hear the birds wake

and looking up
we see dark unveil
their bodies,
the robin's red breast
patient and pulsing,

a pure red.
The maple's black roots
fill with sap,

we gather twigs for kindling.
Chilled and hungry
we continue
with the path, lover and guest,
rearing inside us.

THE GREYHOUNDS

They search for themselves,
not for me

fabric
worn-down
where eyes press:

four white dogs,
one brown

necks craning
toward the scent
which passes —
no use,
the collars restrain them

legs
up to the knee
buried in the flowers.

Richly armed,
men twine two fingers
in their reins,
bravely edging forward,

one pink nose
sniffs the ground
and one the sky.

THE COMMUNITY

1.

Pheasants above me
filtered through *that* water

mouthing it
convinced
its source is different

claws grip
the rim of the fountain

here
where the stream
sets forth

their feathers
drawn back,

    far from flight

not frightened
by what they see
yet

    (face   ?

a cloud
  peering through sunlight ?

half the village
watching them instead).

2.

Sheep nibble the grass
out of nothing more
than boredom

  fat and calmed already

the raccoon
climbs
a sawed-off tree
and meekly sniffs
the top

a bedazzled stag
curls near them,
silver antlers
just below the branches

hairs on the back
of the wolf
stand up on end:

any sudden move
and he will snarl them

panther and civet,
hyena, goldfinch, swallow:

these are
of my family,
point at which
the weaver's hands
fall silent.

CHRONICLE 1

If there were skeptics
yes, you could count me
among them.
Though I can't say
what the others felt.
We pretend to be noble
but it is a fear,
a solemnity which drives us.
We hold our spears carefully
out from our bodies.
We have learned to protect them.
They tell me a crucifix

would be carried much the same.
In the processions.
But I've never seen one.
I say now
that none of us knew
where we were going.
Except possibly the others understood.
I'd best speak for one person only.

LEAVING THE GLEN

Not to Noah's ark
but to a quiet place
within me.
That's where I take two
of every species.
And they learn
to be quiet also.
I imagine them
seated at the table
of my ribs.
Calmly we feed on the huntsmen,
taking their velvet robes
to wrap around us.
Only the hounds
still out there
bay at the moonlight.

FERTILITY RITES

That something is lost
and that something quite different
is followed

Yes but do not disgrace them!
that old man with eyes
half in mud—
he is merely a farmer

and that all this would spring
from his steps
(row after row of corn
interlaced with wheat
when the leap years dictate)

five kernels dropped in together
by so many fingers

burrowing down for the night
let his shadow be stopped there,
he remembers his hand on her body.

HUNTER IN WHITE GOWN

Here I see a man who is also a woman.

He stands three steps in back of the others, his
legs spread apart, the left raised by a rock which
it perches on. His spear is a useless weight across
his shoulder, though he seems not even to feel it.
His cap has fallen too low upon his brow, as if some
force were hidden beneath it. His brown hair curls
wildly at the collar.

Like some child's toy that opens when you press
it, I scream in pain if he stabs me. It should be
clear I'm wounded already, blood running from my
back, my head down and forward, using my horn as a
spear. His friends surround the stream, but don't
dare enter, their dogs pump to stay afloat, too busy
to care about me. It's a game of hide and seek we're
playing: what he's lost is an inner water, flowing
past him. I can drift off in it.

In his right hand he loosely holds the shofar.
This horn of the ram, painted red, edged in gold —
I can see he fears it. He presses it to his lips
and with three fingers guides it upward. His
squinting eyes are noting every movement, whether
of wind or of sunlight. His face expands, like the
face of a man who is drowning. I know he is sounding
it, and yet no sound comes.

CHRONICLE 2

I have seen the one we hunt.
I have sensed his magic.
Not to take him now
would be to let my own life
slip away.
Here by the edge of the stream
we move in and surround him.
It is like the entrance
into heaven:
one of us
will have to pass the test.
We don't know who.
Like the men we are
we take it all into our own hands.
The priests were too slow for us.
Still our spears
even held out to kill
have a sort of reverence.
Some men are crazed from the quest.
Some go through the motions.

TOWARD NO-MAN'S LAND

As if he were rowing a boat,

which is the dog's gut:
these animals
worse off than me.
He stands behind them,
chin and nose
set to attack
if all else fails.
Journeys are carved on his face
by a midwife's fingers.

Two men behind him
angrily turn to each other:
not even those
who have made it across
are this determined.
The poor dogs keep swimming.
It's all they can do
to stay a tenth of an inch
beyond his spear.

Another dog trails at his heels,
having risked nothing.
A rope dangles
from this shepherd's belt,
blurred by each movement:
perhaps some umbilical charm
he assumes is covered.
Other men have hung themselves
with less.

DELIRIUM

He waves goodbye.
I swear it.
The dog that my horn
has just gashed.
The right paws lift
while the left paws balance,
his body folds. . . so long now. . .
take it easy.
Tenderly hands me forgiveness.

CHRONICLE 3

There aren't many people I respect,
but if someone were to ask me now
I would have to tell him
of our leader.
His presence
could give us strength
yet so few of us saw him.
On approaching he held out his hand
to call his dog off
(the dogs were excited and proud;
they had gotten the feel of it).
His eyes showed amazing compassion.
For the dog?
For the men around him?
I couldn't be sure.
More and more
the sense of companionship
overwhelmed me:
friendship
like I'd never known before.
It was about then a woodcutter
spotted our party.
A simple man,
he seemed not to understand us.

DUTY

Always I despised the sight of water.
Now I feel it trickle down my side.

Sacrificed.
The calf gives more
than I do

men pour that blood
into a cup for angels:

deepest red

she drinks
and nobody sees her.

I was born alone,
I hunt from that place in myself
which has known no mother.
A freak a cripple.

THE NOMINATIVE

Horn, or shell

protective
outer constant

singular I
without the dot
or echo.

It is this maiden's
outstretched middle finger
stilled,
pricked by a pin
as she was stitching:

self,
a vanguard by default,
one carries these threads.

A BUTTERFLY, UNSEEN

Was it the life which he dreamt then?

Surely his flight was too short
and half of that time spent
lost in the petals.

I think the petals formed
to cover him.

Because he perches here
where the flower opens
the hunter says that blue specks
on his wings
led themselves to sunlight.

It won't ever be summer always.
And he, having lived a season,
dreams his death.
He's buried in the grass, beneath a shadow.

CHRONICLE 4

So this is the woman they spoke of:
despite her jeweled dress
I say she's common.
Yet even the dogs are subdued.
It's clear that if our prey
is to be captured
it will be here
while her soft hand strokes
and tricks him.
But her fingers come so close.
She could just reach out
and touch that horn.
His power is a kind of gift
we all could share.
There's no need to kill him.
Except we've traveled this far
and we can't turn back.
A man near me sounds the command,
playing half the notes wrong.
All the while he leers at her.
God, how I despise that woman.
Is it normal to hate so?

LESSON

The young dogs gather round
and watch my capture.
Tired bodies strain to keep alert.
They follow the incisions
with their tongues,
soothing me,
washing the blood off.
This is the treat they get
for remaining faithful.
Front row seats.
And tonight the men
feed them grandly.
They will sleep by the fire,
maybe even curl up on the bed.
From my death
they are learning what love is.

MYSTERY

After the hunt I am
placed in damp grass
and the sun falls across me
with a bear's eyes.
On his hind legs
he's taller than I am.

I turn to let my skin
give more to fire.
Honey seeps out of my breasts.

I feed these children.

Softly I lift the heat
out of the water.
Softly a paw's held beside me.

FULL CIRCLE

They say a horse sheds tears
when his master dies

but I am no master;
this finely decked animal
grins as he presents me:

if I should slide from his back,
if I proved my weakness. . .

to be honest with him
while knowing he survives me,
between us is only the wind
no rain for blessing

and I hang my head, casually —

All right,
I toyed with your friendship.
For months I chased you
or your steps
caught up to mine.
Remember, we dunked in a stream
and surfaced
clutching at each others' waists.

We rolled about in a marsh
to warm ourselves,
we forced weeds
to shield us from the sun
which then pursued us.

Brother, your back sweats with fear.
These are those same weeds.

HUNTER AND HUNTED

Spears at our sides,
we bend to rinse our hands.

It's time to eat now.

Dear Lord,
hear his thanks for my flesh,
though he has earned it.
Hear his thanks for my milk
two hours old

listen as both of us
thank you for this woman.
As each man
shares his table with another
he, eating, trusts the fairness
set before him,
her shoulders draped
like two birds, wounded, waking.

The kill stammers inside him.
He recalls a mirage of feathers
turning end on end.
Until you, she, I lay there.
Then he chose to grasp its neck,
not to make it suffer.

I HAVE LAIN DOWN IN THE GRASS, SIR

I see it in your face:
    this is not the answer.

You must brace
your arm on a tree
when you lift that spear.
Hand over hand
you climb toward me:
in your fist the blade is firm,
you let just enough blood flow
to convince them.
You never lowered your eyes
the way the rest did.
Now you try not to raise them.

LAWS OF GRAVITY

Vultures surround the dead.
Or no one here.

What matters?

Falcons sliding down
a lady's arm:
each pecks from a bowl
held out to her.

The morsel given.
Taken.

What does one look for
in hunger?
Any moving thing.
Back of the neck,
bones drawn together:

easy to hang onto.

Then joy for an instant.
A gust of wind
propels me

the open beak snaps
shut between the legs
which spread out
ashamed
as the body retches.

On the ground
he waves the lure
faster and faster
—in a motion of flying,
if he only knew.

Completely in control.
And there is no stopping.
Birds starved then blinded,
trained to return
as always

not to harm but capture.

CHRONICLE 5

Tonight's the first time it's been quiet.
There are no howls from the forest.
Trees gather in tiny groups
to support each other.
As for death,
I find it far too shallow:
the furious reactions
of insane men.
And the dogs react also
though more to the hatred in us
than in themselves.
Often men spend their lives
fearing hell
and then pass through it.
And the man who stayed so calm,
the man I looked up to—
it was he who dealt
the coup de grace.
Seeing that was the worst thing.
Otherwise I might have been convinced.
Blood drips from our spears,
branding us forever.
I think of how heroes display them.

PROCESSION

By nightfall the animals
go to the water again.
But they don't drink.
Peering in too long
they see one who never existed
(and it isn't a stream, it's a river).
I can think of just one word:
friendship.
My mouth gets used to the sound of it.
Then there's another word:
fence.
These posts around me.
The one tree
placed in my enclosure —
strict and whorish
it offers fruit upward.
I draw myself close to its trunk
and I raise my head
in competition.
The base of my paw
scratches ground,
carries some small portion
to my lips.
I am learning, they say, to cooperate.

Typeset at NewComp Graphics Center, a part of
Beyond Baroque Foundation, partially funded by
the National Endowment for the Arts.